LEONARD BERNSTEIN
I HATE MUSIC!
A Cycle of Five Kid Songs

T0085208

CONTENTS

Edited by Richard Walters

Editorial Consultants: Marie Carter, Garth Sunderland

The Name and Likeness of "Leonard Bernstein" is a registered trademark of Amberson Holdings LLC.
Used by Permission.

ISBN 978-1-61780-487-8

LEONARD
BERNSTEIN
Music Publishing
Company LLC

BOOSEY & HAWKES

AN IMAGEM COMPANY

DISTRIBUTED BY

HAL•LEONARD®
CORPORATION
7777 W. BLUEMOUND RD. P.O. BOX 13819 MILWAUKEE, WI 53213

Copyright © 2011 by Boosey & Hawkes, Inc.
All Rights Reserved.

For all works contained herein:
Unauthorized copying, arranging, adapting, recording, Internet posting, public performance,
or other distribution of the printed music in this publication is an infringement of copyright.
Infringers are liable under the law.

www.leonardbernstein.com
www.boosey.com
www.halleonard.com

For Edys

I Hate Music!
A Cycle of Five Kid Songs

(In the performance of these songs, coyness is to be assiduously avoided. The natural, unforced sweetness of child expressions can never be successfully gilded; rather will it come through the music in proportion to the dignity and sophisticated understanding of the singer.)

Words and Music by
LEONARD BERNSTEIN

I. My Name Is Barbara
original key: a major third higher

Copyright © 1943, Warner Bros., Inc. Renewed
Administered by Leonard Bernstein Music Publishing Company LLC
Boosey & Hawkes, Agent for Print.

I don't be-lieve in the storks, ei - ther! ___ They're all in the zoo, bus - y with their own ba - bies! And what's a ba - by - bush, an - y - way!? My name is Bar - ba - ra. ___

II. Jupiter Has Seven Moons

original key: a minor third higher

Copyright © 1943, Warner Bros., Inc. Renewed
Administered by Leonard Bernstein Music Publishing Company LLC
Boosey & Hawkes, Agent for Print.

nine; _____ And ev-'ry one is a lit-tle sun, with six lit-tle moons of its own! _____

Molto meno mosso

mf sadly
But we have on-ly one! Just

poco rit.
think of all the fun we'd have _____ if there were

III. I Hate Music!

original key: a major third higher

Copyright © 1943, Warner Bros., Inc. Renewed
Administered by Leonard Bernstein Music Publishing Company LLC
Boosey & Hawkes, Agent for Print.

IV. A Big Indian and a Little Indian

original key: a major 3rd higher

A big In - di - an and a

lit - tle In - di - an were walk - ing down the street.

Copyright © 1943, Warner Bros., Inc. Renewed
Administered by Leonard Bernstein Music Publishing Company LLC
Boosey & Hawkes, Agent for Print.

V. I'm a Person Too

original key: a major third higher

Copyright © 1943, Warner Bros., Inc. Renewed
Administered by Leonard Bernstein Music Publishing Company LLC
Boosey & Hawkes, Agent for Print.

But ev-'ry-one says, "Is-n't she cute? She likes bal-loons!"

Tempo I *(recovering assertiveness)*

I'm a per-son too, like you!

Tempo II *(simply, by way of explanation)*

I like things that ev-'ry-one likes: I like soft things and mov-ies and hors-es and

warm things and red things: don't you?

Tempo I

mp straightforward

I have lots of thoughts; like what's be - hind the

sky; and what's be - hind what's be - hind the sky: But

Tempo II

ev-'ry-one says, "Is-n't she sweet? She wants to know ev-'ry - thing!" Don't you? Of

16

New York City
March, 1943